Historical Disasters

Pearl Harbor

by Julie Murray

Dash!
LEVELED READERS
An Imprint of Abdo Zoom • abdobooks.com

Dash!
LEVELED READERS

Level 1 – Beginning
Short and simple sentences with familiar words or patterns for children who are beginning to understand how letters and sounds go together.

Level 2 – Emerging
Longer words and sentences with more complex language patterns for readers who are practicing common words and letter sounds.

Level 3 – Transitional
More developed language and vocabulary for readers who are becoming more independent.

THIS BOOK CONTAINS RECYCLED MATERIALS

abdobooks.com

Published by Abdo Zoom, a division of ABDO, PO Box 398166, Minneapolis, Minnesota 55439.

Printed in the United States of America, North Mankato, Minnesota.
052023
092023

Photo Credits: Getty Images, Science Source, Shutterstock
Production Contributors: Kenny Abdo, Jennie Forsberg, Grace Hansen, John Hansen
Design Contributors: Candice Keimig, Neil Klinepier

Library of Congress Control Number: 2022947148

Publisher's Cataloging in Publication Data

Names: Murray, Julie, author.
Title: Pearl harbor / by Julie Murray
Description: Minneapolis, Minnesota : Abdo Zoom, 2024 | Series: Historical disasters | Includes online resources and index.
Identifiers: ISBN 9781098281243 (lib. bdg.) | ISBN 9781098281946 (ebook) | ISBN 9781098282295 (Read-to-me ebook)
Subjects: LCSH: Disasters--Juvenile literature. | History--Juvenile literature. | Pearl Harbor (Hawaii), Attack on, 1941--Juvenile literature.
Classification: DDC 940.5426--dc23

Table of Contents

Pearl Harbor

On December 7, 1941, the Imperial Japanese naval forces attacked the United States naval base at Pearl Harbor.

Pearl Harbor is located on the Hawaiian island of Oahu. In 1908, Naval Station Pearl Carbor was established by the US Navy.

CANADA
UNITED STATES
MEXICO
HAWAIIAN ISLANDS (U.S.)
Pearl Harbor
N
W
E
S
HAWAIIAN ISLANDS

8

In 1940, Pearl Harbor became the permanent base of the United States Pacific **Fleet**. The goal was to show force in the Pacific region.

However, Japan wanted total control of the Pacific. It had to take out US military strength in the area. The easiest way to do this would be with an **aerial attack**.

Mitsubishi A6M "Zero"
A long-range carrier-based fighter aircraft used in the attack on Pearl Harbor.

The Attack

Japan secretly planned the attack for months. At 7:55 a.m. on Sunday, December 7, 1941, the plan became a reality.

Without warning, 350 Japanese planes bombed Pearl Harbor. The attack lasted less than two hours.

UNITED ST
TO THE MEMORY OF
HERE ENTOMBED AN
WHO GAVE THEIR
ON DECEMBER 7, 1941
MADA DE CHILE

In the end, bombers hit 19 US Navy ships, including 8 battleships. More than 300 aircraft were damaged or destroyed. More than 2,400 military personnel were killed and another 1,000 were injured.

The attack changed the course of WWII. On December 8, 1941, the US declared war on Japan. It joined the **Allied Forces** to fight Japan, Germany, and Italy.

Memorial

Today, the Pearl Harbor National Memorial sits where the USS *Arizona* battleship sank. About 1.8 million people visit the memorial each year.

More Facts

- The USS *Arizona* is the final resting place for most of the 1,177 crewmen killed when the battleship was attacked.
- A total of 68 civilians also died in the attack.
- World War II began in 1939. The US joined in 1941. The war lasted until 1945 when Japan surrendered.

Glossary

aerial attack – an attack by armed planes on a surface target.

Allied Forces – In WWII, an international military coalition formed to oppose the Axis powers. Its principal members by 1941 were the United Kingdom, United States, Soviet Union, and China.

fleet – a group of navy ships under one command.

Index

Online Resources

Booklinks
NONFICTION NETWORK
FREE! ONLINE NONFICTION RESOURCES

To learn more about Pearl Harbor, please visit **abdobooklinks.com** or scan this QR code. These links are routinely monitored and updated to provide the most current information available.